LIVING THINGS

LIVING THINGS
COLLECTED POEMS
ANNE PORTER

FOREWORD BY DAVID SHAPIRO

ZOLAND BOOKS
AN IMPRINT OF STEERFORTH PRESS
HANOVER, NEW HAMPSHIRE

An Altogether Different Language was previously
published in a volume by that same name.

The following poems have appeared in *Commonweal:*
"A Morning Dream," "Burning," "After Psalm 137,"
"Music," "Old in the City," and "Five Wishes."

For information about permission to reproduce
selections from this book, write to:
Steerforth Press L.C., 25 Lebanon Street,
Hanover, New Hampshire 03755

Library of Congress Cataloging-in-Publication Data
Porter, Anne, 1911–
Living things : collected poems / Anne Porter. — 1st ed.
p. cm.
Contains new work as well as her previously published collection:
An altogether different language : poems, 1934–1994.
ISBN 1-58195-216-3 (alk. paper)
ISBN 13 978-1-58195-216-2
1. Christian poetry, American. I. Porter, Anne, 1911–
Altogether different language. II. Title.
PS3566.O6295L58 2006
811'.54—DC22
2005029944

FIRST EDITION

CONTENTS

PART 2

An Altogether Different Language

FOREWORD

Dear Anne,

I have been asked to give some insights about you and your work, as the possibility of telling stories about you and your miraculous poems hover about me. As you may not know, I was in love with your poems when I first heard their lyric sway in a strange copy of *Locus Solus,* a magazine mostly of formal cubist experiments in 1961. But we didn't meet until I had outrageously demanded, or at least requested, that Fairfield paint my wife. You and Fairfield welcomed us to your island, and I fell in love with both of you as my other true parents. On Great Spruce Head Island, filled with the flowers, boats, and trees that Fairfield translated, I saw you constantly at work in your woodstove labors, and I thought of you as the interior of all Fairfield's landscapes. He had painted you often, never so beautifully as the time he placed you near a book perhaps often in your mind, St. Francis's writings. I will always place your poetry next to your own translation of his great, colloquial hymn to creatures.

When I asked in 1972, on that first visit, whether you had bats visiting, you replied, your voice as high and lyrical as Gertrude Stein on disc, "Oh they get into the smallest places. . . . To hide, I just pull up the covers over my head." When Fairfield said that Clement Greenberg painted his own name, green hills, you quickly teased: "But you paint your own name too, fair fields." Fairfield was stopped immediately, and we were all a little stunned that you had so quickly punctured his image. And always, we have met and talked, since 1975 and Fairfield's death, about your daughters, Katie and Lizzie, and about your sons, John, Laurence, and Richard. Again and again, you have impressed upon me that your world includes love in its most ordinary form — family — and you have never complained in your poems or your life for all the work that family has taken. You are known by everyone for your poetry, but as with Emily Dickinson, a tremendous amount of your life has been to welcome the stranger, in a radical hospitality that is now celebrated in many books as a minor fact, but was really part of building an amazing life. You and Fairfield gave us a car for a summer for a dollar, a canoe as a gift, the rooms we most loved upstairs in Southampton. And you gave what was obviously the most intense part of your goodness: your attention.

I have mentioned again and again that to me you were saintly, but you don't like the word. Many others will also issue these bouquets and proclamations. For the most part, we are amazed that you have forgiven so many about you for their difficult times as your guests. Your work always reminds me of Fairfield's last walk with me, when we were discussing your religiosity and even your orthodox religiosity. Fairfield told me, half-jokingly, that if we were to join any church it would have to be the Catholic one of yours—"because they let everyone in." Like you, he hated snobs, despite his ancestry among Brahmins and yours among the Transcendentalists. He told me that day that there was a religion of the world. He knew the world was good, and God was not lurking behind it but was in it. God was not concealed; God was in the light.

Fairfield said something that illuminated your poetry for me. He loved the domestic similes in Homer, and I find them in your work. You do not strain after high things; you illuminate with a detail of botany or art history or anything that makes the humble real. The poets of the last years have sometimes been obsessed by linguistic structures themselves. You too are a wild experimentalist, but like Fairfield you pay attention to the page with something like prayer's thankfulness and yearning and petition. John Ashbery once told me he was amazed at the apostrophes I made to God, "as if a real need were being answered," and this is the need in your poetry.

Fairfield and you together: some may even think that this is heresy. I like to think, however, of the way you decided for years not to show your poems to anyone but friends. I recall that you said, after Fairfield's death, that my petition for you to publish a book was to be put off, because Fairfield came first. You always said that marrying was difficult, because you would never receive those marvelous letters again. Like Frank O'Hara's Personalism, and with only the smallest smile, you knew that poetry and painting were intimate letters.

Your poem for Johnny breaks all our hearts, but even more it is rare to find a poet whose ego is so radiant that I had to trick you into publishing your first book, *An Altogether Different Language*, and I was ashamed of it. The story is that I told myself I needed to see your poems all together. I asked you whether you could give me a January birthday present of all that you had. Instead of refusing, which I feared would happen, you said: "Oh good, and that will be very good for my children to see." And so I received the manuscript, was amazed by its virtue, and had my dear friend Larry Weider type it lovingly, and sent it immediately abroad to a publisher. My encounter with one editor, who replied when I said you were perhaps the greatest living Catholic or religious poet, "Why then, forget it," which was a fateful error, has not troubled me overmuch. You were published in a beautiful way and were nominated by the National Book Award jury. And I have always felt that this book and Fairfield's paintings go a long way toward explaining what is spiritual, a hateful word to some like our old friend Kenneth Koch, because he so feared false piety. He loved your work, because it had the variety and brindled skin of his favorite Gerard Manley Hopkins. Kenneth Koch understood that you were "already burning," already a true visionary.

Now few expected *An Altogether Different Language* to grow, but your way is not to stop. Rabbi Terphon said, "It is not ours to finish the work but also not ours to abandon it." So you have gone on, since your work was never about prizes or fame, which you directly indicted. Your work has gone on, like a Chinese painter with the most stringent standards and the subtlest colors. Tu Fu was a favorite of your husband's; I find in you that "pang of hope" that painter-poet Fairfield loved and drew in his most melancholy moods. You can not be called innocent, except in the humility of all your knowledge of "The gem-encrusted church / Of imperial Russia / That bore the holiness / Of Russia's poor / Like an old tree in flower." You bridge many difficulties, and you quote from the Jewish tradition of Abraham Joshua Heschel, whose "moral grandeur and spiritual audacity" you represent. You, like him, cheer us

— just as he cheered a minister who was ashamed of divorce. I have told you of problems, to which you responded: "St. Francis rolled in the snow." I wondered why. You replied: "To get rid of unwanted thoughts." Though you live in a supernatural world, you also speak of it being sufficient "without any miracle." That is why you and Fairfield are our great realists without gentility or cant. Love is often characterized falsely, but to you it is "down-to-earth and practical." I think in this letter I can say that your poems are true gifts. You are not one of the poets in "noble competition," as Kenneth used to say, quoting Nietzsche. That is fine, but you are an example of the joys of influence. And you influence all who come close to you. In you there are the faces of a dozen little Mexican children you describe. Instead of complex formalism, you simply come upon "an antlered stag," and it turns out to be the "ordinary neighborhood" of a toy and of benevolence. Boxwood bushes have never been extolled this way, like a Bellini: "When sun is on them / They yield a double perfume / Of fresh-ground coffee and the musk / Of certain mushrooms that are found / Growing wild in pastures."

Fairfield used to go with me through the Metropolitan Museum and other galleries, and he said he was looking for light. Did Eakins have light? No, it was too scientific too often. But even the sculls? No, it was not light. Did this man or that man have light? No. Light was something that could be found in the most radical post-Impressionists, for example, or in Tintoretto. It was an envelope between us, and it was the radiance of paint itself. You have light, Anne, you *have* light. And a turtle is full of the Hebrew alphabet in your poems, and you yourself are burning in another. I know you *believe,* in an age that welcomes skepticism. Fairfield himself said to me that though a poet we loved, John Ashbery, had teased him: "What does ultimate reality mean?" Fairfield agreed with me that this reality of light was *in* the world, again not concealed. Ashbery was a religious poet. Many spoke in the twentieth century and continue to speak today of the hidden, of the *deus absconditus.* But that is not your way. For you God is not concealed but is the world. You might be called, but by accident, a Spinozist, a person who is an acosmist, for whom only God exists. But you know that the smallest things are radiant, as when your mother is quoted about the newborn: "I love their little mottled arms." Kenneth loved your work, because it was personal, various, and surprising, because even in the poem to your wounded child Johnny you have the humor and changeable mood that is the opposite of frozen dogma. Like the greatest painters, you have developed your own light, not behind everything but in everything.

DJS
Riverdale, New York
2005

P.S. You will forgive me for not making the metrical, structural, and other critiques that will show your relationship, for example, to the nature poetry in James Schuyler, whom you took in and also subtly influenced. I leave that task for normal critics, who may learn a lot from your pluralism. But in this letter, I am bold enough to say, as when I first told you that everyone would love to read your poems, this book with your continuing creativity is itself a translation of Francis in life and art, a love letter to Fairfield. Your poems are humble as water and radiant in the smile that discloses each creature in your maternal gaze. How blessed I am, how lucky to have known you and your family of poets. Your poetry is "already burning."

FOREWORD TO
An Altogether Different Language

This is a shocking book, for all its seeming diffidence, economy, and quietness. In the twentieth century, we are used to poets of skepticism and the subjunctive, from Hardy to Stevens; and we are certainly accustomed to poets of the worldly surface, from Apollinaire to O'Hara. We are perhaps most habituated to the poetry that confesses a separation from the transcendental, and T.S. Eliot himself went so far as to underline how often it is just this that convinces us: the cry of separation. However, we cannot forget how much of modernity is a spiritual art, and the sacred is what Rimbaud and Mondrian and Le Corbusier thirsted for in their radical work. If we have problems, because so much of the language of belief has grown connotatively encrusted, then we wait for the poets who believe enough and can freshen this dialect.

Anne Porter is one of the rare poets who believes enough, who lives in days and holidays, and who has stunningly found a language to transmit her Franciscan joy in created things. Her diction is as modest as that of William Carlos Williams or of a poet she nurtured as a houseguest for many years, James Schuyler. She has a particular Negative Capability for speaking for the speechless: the poor, the peddler, the homeless, the sick. Her portrait of Anastasia shows how she escapes "Blue Period" sentimentality while she does this, as when she is willing to notice the stain of anti-Semitism in her protagonist. She once said, "We were built for heaven, like a boat," and her poetry has both a child-like flow and a rugged confidence. Her nature-worship might remind one of her Channing family's tradition of New England transcendentalism, but she has a rare willingness to be canonical: "Easter is growing / in the paschal moon / Like a child in its mother." The poet is certain, not only because a map has been given, but because she is willing to travel without maps, and look, and be amazed.

She takes the side of things, of living things, and of the creator. Is her work a long series of commentaries on scripture? No, because it is observed and biographical: "While the tiny maple leaves are curling like birds' feet round the frost / Through all the whispering to you in buses as I ride to see grandchildren . . ." From the earliest formal poems to the latest, she gives us a practiced poetry of wonder: "Now the smallest creatures, who do not know they have names," and she finds the connections between names and natural things. She is unembarrassed by ordinary, even sordid detail, as in the "sweaty gowns" that stick to the patients in her *In a Country Hospital.* And if one thinks she is merely pious or reticent, she finds gigantic depths and tumult, as in *Consider the Lilies of the Sea:* "Death sprung open in a depth of sea." Her faith has enlarged her, not the reverse, and her poetry has the grandeur of seeing things "as if for the first time." It is not surprising to be reminded of the Surrealists in this sacred art of the everyday: "They sing / In breaking waves / And rock like wooden cradles."

She has the quality of paying attention to ultimate reality that Fairfield Porter, who painted her so often alone and with their five children, told me should be the conclusion of every sermon. She also knows, like that great painter of "light and repose," that ultimate reality is in everything and not lurking behind it. In her most poignant poem, for her son Johnny, she gives us an amazing cadenza of his problems, his jokes ("In heaven the angels kid and joke"), and his anxieties. This poem is as well-written as prose and also as song. It has the purity of Apollinaire or Eluard and is filled with the audacious Pop-Art vividness of unembarrassed life. Only a great poet could control this poem of suffering without bathos, and its loving details illuminate for us a whole open house.

Her elegant poem on the circus reminds us that Anne Porter has kept her talent for seeing the world as "one big surprise." She keeps her eyes open, from Denver to Albuquerque, and sees the funny graffiti: "LOVE IS AMONG US," in the dirty washroom. Like Schuyler, she takes the side of flowers and is "beyond flowers," at once a poet of immanence and exaltation: "No one will see the day-lilies / The color of red foxes, / Waist-high coarse-textured lilies." Though some might be misled into thinking this poetry naive, it is gently learned, as when she can suddenly apostrophize the poet and the painter on familiar terms: "Walt Whitman honored you,

Jean-Francois Millet . . . And I thank you myself." But it is the gratitude, one must say the Franciscan gratitude, that remains. Her greatest emotional perspective is that of praise: "You saved it for us out of that warm life / Which God has hidden somewhere."

These poems are as powerful as secrets, as "secret praise / Which burns in every creature." They give us the feeling of a complete art, a mature poet, who has the resilient gift of translating seemingly non-verbal, non-sensuous states into sensuous poetry. We accept these "parables of the kingdom," because they are given to us as ordinary and possible perspectives, not obscurities. Though she recognizes irreducible evils, her poetry tends to burst into clarity, as in her amazing poem of oaks and squirrels, and *A Biography of Flowers,* with its microscopy, and the masterful image of dissemination in *The Pear Tree:* "Disclosing every tender filament / Sticky with nectar / Beaded with black pollen." This poetry is so refined that it might be thought of as innocent, but will, like her Sarah in *Another Sarah,* become: "A wave of living sweetness / A nation of white petals / A dynasty of apples." These last refinements make her an ecstatic exception, an American religious poet of stature who reminds us that the idea of the holy is still possible for us.

This poetry is filled with domesticity and family — the poet raised five children while taking care of countless others, myself included — but it is also filled with the widest world, from Long Island to Assisi, of material and immaterial spaces and history. Her poetry has digested all variety of traditional influences and seems in this complete volume unmistakable and independent. We are led to the conclusion of Laurance Wieder and others that she is among the superb poets of the sacred in this century, though her subtly assertive work directs praise elsewhere. Fairfield Porter broke the taboos of his age against representing nature and figure, while still loving gesture and color. Anne Porter, with her own sense of liberty and courage, breaks our secular taboo against representing invisible love, while still praising and defining living things in clearest tones.

For Anne Porter, the holy is found in a commitment to Christ the Mediator and his triumph in suffering for a suffering world. However, she gives a constant, almost pantheistic pressure to the theme that the Kingdom of God is within and without, so that her radiant if concise imagism is all in the service of God. This paradox reminds us that for Pound, a squirrel was just that particular squirrel, but that for Anne Porter, concrete creatures also run into "invisible arks," as we are all part of "warring disobedient history." That is, the concrete is also part of an unruined allegory that harmonizes. It is her oscillation between the literal, symbolic, allegorical, and even anagogic worlds that gives her sparse poetry its strange richness. With the publication of these poems, American poetry is suddenly and substantially enriched.

DAVID SHAPIRO

PART 1

In Another World

A FAMINE CHILD

You had no food today
And may have none tomorrow
Child whose ribs are showing
Under your dark skin

Unwilling to be wounded
By the sight
Of so unjust a hunger

Or to confront the anger
Of the Lord who made you

We look away
We turn away our faces.

SAINT MATTHEW'S WEEDS

Matthew 13, 29–30

The revolutionaries came
With justice and injustice
Saying "The Revolution
Is all we need of God."

The men and women who
Were still believers
Evil and good alike
They drove into the cold
Siberian wilderness

They swept away the Church
With all its human failures
The gem-encrusted church
Of imperial Russia

That bore the holiness
Of Russia's poor
Like an old tree in flower.

THE ICON

Here in this icon out of ancient Russia
Brown as amber the little Mother of God
Holding her Infant to her cheek
Is present to us
In all her wise
And peaceful sorrow

A forest hermit painted this
They say at night his face
Lit up the snow

He befriended robbers
And often gave
The bears his bread.

AN ONLY SON

Out of the world
Of tents and sheep
A legend has come down
The story of a rabbi's only son
Who when his childhood ended
Left his father

To live like one who's disinherited
Hungry disheveled and alone
To work as a day laborer
To wander through the desert or the mountains
Where finding others poorer than himself
He'd gather sticks for them and haul their water
He'd play at children's games among their children
And sleep outdoors at night

His father said
At night I lie awake
Grieving about my son
Who has no flocks or herds
Or wife or child
And for possessions
Only a knife
A blanket and a cup

But he is single-hearted
And the Lord
Blesses the single-hearted
He prefers
Their frailty

He prefers their sins
To the good works
And virtues of the arrogant.

—FROM *Moral Grandeur and Spiritual Audacity,*
P. 63, BY RABBI ABRAHAM JOSHUA HESCHEL

ADAM'S FALL

None of the animals feared me, I'd given them all their names,
At night I fell asleep with my head on the lion's flank,
All day I did nothing but sing, there was an abundance of fruit,
I had only to hold out my hand,
and the Lord would fill it with bread.

But when I woke up this morning there was no garden around me,
I was lying alone with Eve on the hard ground
And we were hungry, but there was nothing to eat.
The animals wouldn't come to us anymore,
And where the door to the garden had been, there was nothing
    but fire.

THE ROOFS OF PARIS

In the year 1900
More or less
Vuillard the painter
Finished a little landscape
That he called
The Roofs of Paris

There's the gray pearl
Of the Parisian sky
Black chimney pots
And scaly-slated gables
Whose stormy gray
Is tinged with violet

Beyond them and above them
Are the mansard roofs

High in the crusty russet
Of their roofing-tiles
Vuillard has painted
A dormer window where
Like a white crocus
Blooms
The figure of a child
In a white smock.

ATTIC WINDOWS

I live in a neighborhood
Of three-storey wooden houses
And in their highest gables
Right up under the eaves
Are small odd-shaped windows
That I never notice
Till suddenly one evening
They fill up with light
And I know that my neighbor's children
Are home for the holidays

These are the windows
Of those attic bedrooms
With rough rafters
Rooms that are either
Too hot or too cold
They may contain a drum-set
Or an empty birdcage
Or a broken chair
Even a honeycomb the bees
Abandoned in the rafters
They're rooms needed only
When every child is home

Only on holidays
And maybe close to midnight
A light in a triangular
Or round or fan-shaped window
Will all at once appear
Shining above the trees

It gives off a flash of wonder
Like a child's first word
Or a singer touching her highest
Most beautiful note of all.

OLD IN THE CITY

You grow geraniums
And crochet baby-bonnets
But you walk slowly
Every day more slowly
As if there were a rock
In your poor belly

You stay away from doctors
They'd send you to the hospital
Where pieces are cut out of you
And after that you die

Instead you walk to the park
Where there are oaks and elm trees
That stream up to the sun
With triumph in their branches

Where there's a secret nation
Of squirrels who find it convenient
To set up their nests in the treetops
Like vendors who set up their stalls
By the steps of a great cathedral

And sometimes you sit in the playground
Waiting for the children
Who come when school is out

They rush in all together
Throwing their books on the benches
And racing to the swings

Over and over again
Their feet in their battered sneakers
Fly up into the air
And their hair too is flying
A wordless and intent
Delight is in their faces.

PROPHETS

Once in the Advent season
When I was walking down
A narrow street

I met a flock of children
Who all came running up to me
Saying that they were prophets
And for a penny they
Would prophesy

I gave them each a penny

They started out
By rummaging in trash-cans
Until they found
A ragged piece of silk

It's blue, they said
Blue is a holy color
Blue is the color that
The mountains are
When they are far away

They laid the rag
On a small fire
Of newspaper and shavings
And burned it in the street

They scraped up all the ashes
And with them decorated
Each other's faces

Then they ran back to me
And stood
In a circle 'round me

We stood that way
In a solemn silence
Until
One of the children spoke

It was the prophecy!

He said that long before
The pear tree blossoms
Or sparrows in the hedges
Begin to sing

A Child will be our King.

EMMETT KELLY

Once at the circus
In Philadelphia
I saw Emmett Kelly
The famous clown

Dressed as a tramp
Unshaven
A big sad clown-face
Painted on

He wandered vaguely out
Onto the circus floor
His lunch-box in his hand

The band was playing
And the huge spangled
Elephants were dancing
The bareback riders
Were turning cartwheels on the backs
Of whirling horses
And there were tigers plunging
Through hoops of fire

He took no notice of it

Instead he picked a spot
Right in the thick of it
And carefully sat down

And then with a majestic
Simplicity
Like that of the great apes

He took a sandwich
Out of his lunch-box
And munched it slowly

And then he slowly peeled
And ate an apple

He took a drink
Out of a soda bottle
And wiped his mouth
With his bandana

Then he stood up
And brushed the sawdust from his pants
And shuffled off
Into the nearest exit

And that was all.

THE WINGÉD CHILDREN

Once when my friends
Were driving through the desert
In Mexico

They passed a pickup truck
And in the back of it

Each with a pair of wings
Of sky-blue plush

Such as is used
For making bedroom-slippers

There rode a dozen little
Mexican children.

SUMMER COTTAGE

This is a house
That smells of melons and roses
Sea-wind pours through it
The airy curtains float
And the wiry sprays
Of the sea-lavender
Tremble on the table

The hushed roar
Of the massive ocean
Covers us night and day
It shelters us
Like a tree shadow
We live in it
As in a forest.

THE TRAVEL-PICTURES

This is the mountaintop
Clouds' castle, eagles' nest
And granite cradle
Of a great river

And here's a lavish
Heap of cloud
In pure blue sky
A feature of this country

This is the fresh
And glowing green
Of snow-fed grasses
In a steep mountain pasture
Where sheep and lambs are grazing

This is a mountain farmer
And his bride
Here you can see
Their country faces
And his ill-fitting suit
Her heavy satin
Borrowed for their wedding

They leave the church on horseback
The bride's long veil is flying

And here she's throwing
The beggar children
Her bouquet of roses

And here's a harsh archaic
Wayside Calvary
That's blotched with lichen

Here are some gypsy children
They're decorating it
With empty soda-cans
And rows of pebbles

Here's an old man
Drunk or asleep beside it
On the bare ground

A small black dog
Is guarding him

Later we learned
That the dog's name is Balthazar
And he has one blue eye

Here is a living
Cypress-tree
"Planted the year
The Lord was born"
A gypsy told us

The children
Are peeling off
Some strips of bark
They braid them into baskets

This is a bloodstained rabbit
Hanging head-downwards from a peg
Outside a poacher's hut

Stuck in the wall beside it
Is the skinning-knife

And here's an acre of
Sweet lavender
And here's an almond-orchard
That's all in flower

This is a fishing village
In the evening twilight
Lamplight in cottages
The fleet at anchor

Luster of evening
On the harbor water
And in the dusky heavens
Hesperus shining.

NOËL

When snow is shaken
From the balsam trees
And they're cut down
And brought into our houses

When clustered sparks
Of many-colored fire
Appear at night
In ordinary windows

We hear and sing
The customary carols

They bring us ragged miracles
And hay and candles
And flowering weeds of poetry
That are loved all the more
Because they are so common

But there are carols
That carry phrases
Of the haunting music
Of the other world
A music wild and dangerous
As a prophet's message

Or the fresh truth of children
Who though they come to us
From our own bodies

Are altogether new
With their small limbs
And birdlike voices

They look at us
With their clear eyes
And ask the piercing questions
God alone can answer.

ON A MAINE ISLAND

Fog pours into the sprucewood
And now they're all printed in dew
Cobwebs all over the moss
We never knew were there!

A SHORT PRAYER

Mary, in you
We see the flowering
Of our human beauty
And hear
The songs of God

And in your heart the lost
Rejected and abandoned ones
Are held in honor

Stay with us now
And always.

SIGNS AND WONDERS

The winter must be over
At five o'clock this morning
I heard the wood-dove's call
Four notes and then a pause
And then another four
Soft as a sea-wind blowing
Into an empty bottle

Flocks of wingéd snowdrops
Dangle trembling
From fine-spun stalks
Under leafless hedges

And late last night we saw
A strangeness in the sky
A long dim skein of light
Beside the Little Dipper

It was Hyatukaké
The spring comet
Stella Comata
Is its other name
The long-haired star
Flying through the heavens
Veiled in silver

Ranging so far
It slips behind the sun
Is gone for generations

Astronomers have told us
That in another spring
When ten millennia have passed
It will be seen again.

A SONG OF FEAR AND FIRE

If when I die
Instead of going off to Purgatory
As I hope to do
I have become a tiny flake of ash
Still glowing with the spark
Of life you gave me

And if I'm tossed
Into a fearful nothingness
Beyond the stars
There to go whirling
Whirling round
Until my fire goes out

Until my fire goes out
I still will praise you.

A SAFE NEIGHBORHOOD

Shopkeepers bankers poets contractors
Watering quiet lawns
And sleeping
In heated houses

If even here
Some ordinary grief can knife our hearts
Down to the very quick

How is it for those others?
Famine is their nourishment
Rubble of war their garden
A freezing wind their home.

A DESERT GRANDCHILD

for Guru-Sahai

I came here late at night
And I'm lying awake on a cot
In the laundry-room of a house
At the edge of Navajo country

For now it's a house full of sleep
With a still desert around it
And the still glory of the stars
Fills the black sky above it

There must be a cuckoo clock
In another room somewhere
I'm counting its wooden hiccups
And now I hear a child

It must be my son's child
Frightened by a dream
She's calling her foster-parents
Her voice shines in the dark.

THE ERMINE WEASEL

Slim as a lizard
The little ermine weasel
Is hunted in the winter
When her pelt is white

But she turns brown in summer
And in an earthen burrow
Under a pasture stone
Her kits are born

With her wild milk
She suckles them
Until their teeth are cut
And then she brings them pheasants
Larger than herself

And carries in her innocence
And creature passion
That secret other poetry
Which never will be written.

TERRY BERRIGAN

The seven years we lived
On 52nd Street
We had a neighbor
Terry Berrigan
Who was the playmate
Of our youngest son

Terry was one of eight
Most of them boys
Who ran all through
The neighborhood
Dodging the trucks
And scattering the sparrows

Gap-toothed and freckle-faced
With ears
A size too big
Terry was little
For a boy of seven

His Irish mother told him
Terry you're so small
That if the devil
Should ever catch you
He'd throw you back
For sure
He's got no use at all
For little minnows

✧　✧　✧

In my last year
On 52nd Street
When all the world around us
Was steeped in war
Terry and I
Each had a war at home

For Terry had
His drunken father
And my own house was filled
With anger and confusion

And Terry understood
I was in trouble
One day he brought me
A child-size plastic medal
On a scrap of ribbon
And in his husky brogue
He said it was the nuns
Had got it for him
He said it had
A blessing on it
And I should keep it always
And that was all he said

✧　　✧　　✧

After we moved away
From 52nd Street
I had no news of Terry
But I kept his medal
In a cracked saucer
On a pantry shelf

One day I picked it up
And looked at it
Intently in a way
I hadn't looked before

And there in front of me
Was Terry's Mary
And her wide-open hands
That streamed with blessings.

— IN GRATEFUL MEMORY
OF PATRICIA CUFFE
WHO WAS MY FRIEND IN IRELAND

FIVE WISHES

I'd like to have a wild bird
Perch on my hand
A sparrow or
A chickadee
Sudden with her sharp feet
And fragile daring

I'd like to see again
The etchings Rembrandt made
Of stories from the Bible

Though they're as plain
As Bethlehem's hay
A radiance fills them

And I would like to visit
The Laguna Indians
And their old church
Made of whitewashed clay
With logs for rafters

And in it their Madonna
To whom they've given
A white lace apron

And I would like to learn
To accept my death
To accept our dying
That strange dawn

So deeply scandalous
That God himself wept
At the death of his friend

I'd like to find
The shrine of Chimayo
Where the lame leave crutches

I'd like to go there
With my daughter Katie

It would be enough
Just to be there
Without any miracle.

A PARADE IN THE CITY

It was a morning
In early May
Trees were in infant leaf
When on our street we heard
A pounding in the air
And it grew stronger

Till all at once
There poured into the street
Out of another neighborhood

A little dazzling
Holy Day parade

First came the drummers
And the trumpeters

The drums were painted with tulips
And brightly colored birds

There followed several rows
Of children marching
In scarlet jackets stiff
With gold embroidery

Next came a pickup truck
And in the back of it
Under a rainbow-colored canopy
Of paper streamers
Rode the smaller children
Solemn in their headdresses
Of ribbons and flowers

And then there came
The image of Our Lady
Of Czestokowa
With her brown face
And with a sword-cut in her cheek
From one of the long wars

Crowned and robed in jewels
Holding her Child
She rode slowly past us
On a float filled with daisies

There were some older children
In festive peasant costume
Who danced along beside her
And sometimes they were walking
On their hands
And sometimes turning cartwheels

And last of all
There came three strong old men
In sober Sunday clothing

Then the parade was gone
Leaving behind it in the street
A sudden emptiness of lost
Astonishment
Still faintly throbbing.

THREE BIRDS

Song-sparrows

Our sudden blissful
Lisping songs
Are quickly over

But they are long enough
For us who are so small

Crows

The crows fly through the woods
Like heavy shadows
Of other birds which are
Themselves invisible

The Song of the Thrush

Inside the thrush's song
There is another

A flash of dissonance
That's like thin crystal breaking
And ringing as it breaks.

BOXWOOD

When one is very old
And close to dying
There are so many fellow-creatures
To say good-bye to

For instance
There are the boxwood bushes
Dense and symmetrical they thrive
In venerable gardens

Their tiny waxen leaves
Are highly polished
And of a green so deep
It's nearly black

When sun is on them
They yield a double perfume
Of fresh-ground coffee and the musk
Of certain mushrooms that are found
Growing wild in pastures.

A MORNING DREAM

Towards morning
In a shallow sleep
I dreamed a dream

About a small black woman
Who somehow
Sat facing me
In a wooden chair

Her hands
Were resting in her lap
Her face was seamed
With poverty and age
And she was wearing
A dark blue Sunday dress
With a print of roses

She had been reading us
Passages from the Gospels
And it was beautiful
The way she read them
I thanked her for it

Sometimes I read like that
She said
It's from the Lord.

A PAINTER'S LIFE

When I was twelve years old
I came upon the paintings
Of one who was a misfit like myself
A lonely awkward man

He painted shaggy whirling stars
As big as suns
And sunflowers with tawny manes
As fierce as lions
He painted fields ablaze
With yellow wheat

And then his narrow bedroom
His bandaged face
And some old work-boots
That he portrayed with reverence and care
Like one who is transcribing
A letter from the Lord

He painted portraits
Of his village neighbors
In order to belong to them
To be enfolded in their life
Like the village doctor

He painted them
With his most radiant colors

"I wanted haloes for them"
He told his brother.

A TURTLE'S SHELL

I found a turtle dead
Trapped in a dry well
Gone was her scaly body
And there was only the hollow
Dome of her black shell
Strong as a monument

It had an indecipherable
Yellow message
Painted all over it
In figures not unlike
The Hebrew alphabet.

BURNING

There is a hidden kind
Of humble goodness
I love in others

Only an aeon
Of refining fire
Could make it mine

But sometimes it's as if
I were already burning.

IN ANOTHER WORLD

The twentieth century began
A second decade
When I began my life
Large patches of the former century
Still lay about
Like snow in April

Cities were quiet
Though often in the night
The tomcats quarreled
The sounds by day
Were the clip-clop
Of horses' feet
The chirp of sparrows
And in the alleys
RAGS BONES AND BOTTLES
The ragman's cry

Lumber and coal
And gravel, bricks and stones
Were hauled in wooden wagons
By teams of slow
Colossal horses

The streams were clear
The forests all around us
Were deep and strong
And few believed
That Nature could be wounded.

A PLEA FOR MERCY

When I am brought before the Lord
What can I say to him
How plead for mercy?

I'll say I loved
My husband and the five
Children we had together
Though I was most unworthy

I'll say I loved
The summer mornings
I loved the way the sun comes up
And sets the dew on fire
I loved the way
The cobwebs shine
On the tall grass
When they are strung with dew

I'll say I loved
The way that little bird
The titmouse flies
I'll say I loved
Its lightness
Lilt
And beauty.

THE SONG OF THE WREN

At half past four in the morning
My neighbor the brown wren
Whose nest is in the woodshed
Begins his delicate song

It rambles on and on
Jig for a tiny fiddle
Squeak in the rusty wheels
Of a rickety elfin cart
Wobbling toward the sun.

STELLA RAPKOWSKI

Making the Stations of the Cross
In the small wooden church
Built for themselves
By Polish immigrants

Stella Rapkowski
The ninety-year-old mother
Of a local
Potato-farmer

Whispers her prayers in Polish
And moves like the hand of a clock
From Station to Station

She is the steadfast little
Sister of the sun
Her every morning
Is a faithful copy
Of all her other mornings.

THE MASTER OF MARY OF BURGUNDY

Late in the Middle Ages
An unknown master painter
Made an illuminated
Book of Hours
Painted on parchment
For Marie de Bourgoyne
Who was his patron

Intact and radiant
His little book survives
At a museum in London

It is an offering
Of cornflowers and carnations
Pea-blossoms columbines
Curly acanthus leaves
And Johnny-jump-ups
Forget-me-nots wild forest strawberries
And the flat pink and white
Daisies of Europe

There is a page of skulls
For All Souls' Day
A still life of two bowls
One of red currants
One of black
Whose meaning
Has been forgotten
A page of pearls is followed by
A page of peacock-feathers
And through a window in a wall
Of cockleshells
We see the Crucifixion

Not crushed or smothered
As if caught in amber
But fresh as if alive
There is a ladybug a dragonfly
A bee a worm a snail

And butterflies
Are everywhere
It is an offering
Of butterflies
The Saffron and the Tortoiseshell
The Meadow Brown
And the Small Cabbage White

Between these teeming margins
Mary of Burgundy
Could peep
At a divine
Stillness in tiny landscapes
Where stories
Of our life with God
Appear in burning blue
And red and gold

It is an offering of gold

Around a salutation to
The Blessed Virgin
Beginning
I beseech you
Obsecro te

The painter spread
A border of pure gold
Sprinkled with violets

And with them three
Brown spotted butterflies
A kind still common in the woods
Of the Ardennes near Brussels.

SUSANNA

Nobody in the hospital
Could tell the age
Of the old woman who
Was called Susanna

I knew she spoke some English
And that she was an immigrant
Out of a little country
Trampled by armies

Because she had no visitors
I would stop by to see her
But she was always sleeping

All I could do
Was to get out her comb
And carefully untangle
The tangles in her hair

One day I was beside her
When she woke up
Opening small dark eyes
Of a surprising clearness

She looked at me and said
You want to know the truth?
I answered Yes

She said it's something that
My mother told me

There's not a single inch
Of our whole body
That the Lord does not love

She then went back to sleep.

AFTER PSALM 137

We're still in Babylon but
We do not weep
Why should we weep?
We have forgotten
How to weep

We've sold our harps
And bought ourselves machines
That do our singing for us
And who remembers now
The songs we sang in Zion?

We have got used to exile
We hardly notice
Our captivity
For some of us
There are such comforts here
Such luxuries

Even a guard
To keep the beggars
From annoying us

Jerusalem
We have forgotten you.

MUSIC

When I was a child
I once sat sobbing on the floor
Beside my mother's piano
As she played and sang
For there was in her singing
A shy yet solemn glory
My smallness could not hold

And when I was asked
Why I was crying
I had no words for it
I only shook my head
And went on crying

Why is it that music
At its most beautiful
Opens a wound in us
An ache a desolation
Deep as a homesickness
For some far-off
And half-forgotten country

I've never understood
Why this is so

But there's an ancient legend
From the other side of the world
That gives away the secret
Of this mysterious sorrow

For centuries on centuries
We have been wandering
But we were made for Paradise
As deer for the forest

And when music comes to us
With its heavenly beauty
It brings us desolation
For when we hear it
We half remember
That lost native country

We dimly remember the fields
Their fragrant windswept clover
The birdsongs in the orchards
The wild white violets in the moss
By the transparent streams

And shining at the heart of it
Is the longed-for beauty
Of the One who waits for us
Who will always wait for us
In those radiant meadows

Yet also came to live with us
And wanders where we wander.

THE SWALLOWS' FLIGHT

The warmth of summer is
Our dwelling-place
And summer is our home
It is a floating and
A flowing country
To live in it
We have to travel with it

When autumn has begun
And nights grow longer
We launch our flock on the invisible stream
That bears us through the winding
Mountain passes
This way and that until
The mountains are behind us
Their flowers withered
And their aspens golden

We're in the tropics now
A fiery sun is glowing
And the trees
Have leathery big leaves

The southwind sweeps us high
Into the stormy air
Above the jungle
Our wings are heavy
With the drenching rain
Again and yet again
We're beaten backwards
And some of us are lost

Bewildered and exhausted
We continue flying
Above a jungle river
Late in the afternoon
We see beneath us
The tawny rooftops
Of our promised village

As if it were the gesture
Of a single creature
We slant our wings and then
Come swirling down
Into the village streets

Twittering we alight
On roofs and treetops
On hedges gates and arches
Even the little belfry
Of the Angelus
Is clothed in feathers

The shouting laughing
Village children
Come tumbling out to greet us
And all our desperate long journey
Is lost in joy and utterly forgotten.

PART 2

An Altogether Different Language

CRADLE SONG II

for Leah, Jack & Joshua

The moon is full tonight
The paschal moon
This is the eve of Passover
This is the night
The moon was made for

Like wild grapes in a thicket
When they breathe out their fragrance
The moon gives off her light
A light which is the sun's
Sheer radiant shadow

It overflows
In the deserted streets
The grass is frosted by it
The rooftops glisten

And in the rooms
Where there are children sleeping
The shapes of windows
Cut from thin moonlight
Are shining on the floor

Behind the theater
In an alleyway
A peddler is asleep
Drooping against the wall
And without waking him
The moon
Shines on his cart his shoes
His coat his cap
His sleeping eyelids

Down at the beach
The full moon tide
Is at the flood
The beach has disappeared
Covered with salt water
Driftwood is floating
The coarse beach grass
And silvery herbs
That grow beside the sea
Are standing in salt water

This is the night
For which the moon was made
And she has veiled all creatures
With bridal light
Binding them up together
Into one stillness
Into one silence
Into one sleep

The children asleep in their cots
And the peddler by his cart
The beach grass and the silvery herbs
That stand in the salt water
By the edge of the sea
And the moon's luminous wafer
Lifted up over the trees
Are all bound up together
In that one sleep

And there'll be no division
No separation between them
Until the birds' first rippling cry
At the touch of morning

IN HOLY WEEK

While we're asleep
The paschal moon is shining
High above the trees

And high above the trees
Even while we're sleeping
Easter is growing
In the paschal moon
Like a child in its mother.

THE DREAM

Listen! I saw in dreaming
A hill where no gleaming
Leaves drew life from any tree,
But there was walking close to me
A girl, barefoot among
The thistles and the cow dung.
Bramble and bird were glad
Of a power that she had.
The showery cloud above her head
Hung unshowering, comforted.

Wordless as a wind
She spoke then to my mind
And so showed to me
A charred nunnery
In that hill's valley.
The window sockets stared about
With their brightness all plucked out
And behind these and far within
Wandered lost the weeping wind,
And the lost bird wandering
Battered the dust with his wild wing.

Out of a skull's mouth quietly
Shakes the living butterfly,
Out of a doorway the nuns came
As out of sleep the living dream.
I saw them break into the light,
Eyeless children, veiled with white.
So they came through that door
Behind whose darkness, far within,
The weeping wind was prisoner.

Their holy water was all blood,
All their wreaths were weeds and straw,
But from their mouths, when they sang,
Soundless wings like flowers sprang,
Wings so fresh and so young
They let through the light of the sun,
Out of air such whiteness making
My eyes lost it on awaking.

THE FIRST OF MAY

Now the smallest creatures, who do not know they have names,
In fields of pure sunshine open themselves and sing.
All over the marshes and in the wet meadows,
Wherever there is water, the companies of peepers
Who cannot count their numbers, gather with sweet shouting.
And the flowers of the woods who cannot see each other
Appear in perfect likeness of one another
Among the weak new shadows on the mossy places.

Now the smallest creatures, who know themselves by heart,
With all their tender might and roundness of delight
Spending their colors, their myriads and their voices
Praise the moist ground and every winking leaf,
And the new sun that smells of the new streams.

IN A COUNTRY HOSPITAL

Somewhere in this brick building a woman in labor groans,
The morning is still dark.
But the robins' clamor has started, and the ground-fog is rising,
(I had to get up to look.)
Two lamps at the hospital gate
Paint the green hedge with falseness
And the morning star is shining,
High, clear, fresher than dew
In the transparent wilderness overhead.

Soon day will come, with her plain clattering gold
And linen piled on carts, and smells of ether and coffee
Filling the wards and corridors, and the lamps and the star will
        go out.

We can hear the cries of the newborn, and a man coughing
        without relief,
We can hear sparrows riffling up out of the coolness into the eaves
And chirping there, loud and excited, as if it were their
        market place.

We can hear the roar of the mile-away Atlantic floating beyond
        the town,
Beyond the wheat and potato-fields and the beach-grass
        and the dunes
Beyond the brackish ponds where the swans nest,
A shimmering mountain of praises, of crystal and thunder.

And to us, whose sweaty gowns stick to us,
Who are all twisted, who are all aching,
This Friday morning the blessed Eucharist was brought.

CONSIDER THE LILIES OF THE SEA

Their salt wet life erased, eroded, only
The shells of snails lie on the sand,
Their color darkens toward the whorl's conclusion,
The center is nearly black. Even the fragments
Faithfully observe their tribal custom
Of involution; the motionless whirlpool
Is clearly written on the broken shield.

The two joined petals of a small
Tooth-white clamshell stand ajar, and mimic
The opening of wings or of a songbook;
Leaves that a minute and obscure
Death sprung open in a depth of sea;
Held in one's hand, they still present
The light obedient gesture that let go of time.

And close to these frail, scattered, and abandoned
Carvings which were the armor and the art
Of dark blind jellies that the fish have eaten,
The big Atlantic cumulates and pours,
Flashes, is felled, and streaks among the pebbles
With wildfire foam.

LIVING THINGS

Our poems
Are like the wart-hogs
In the zoo
It's hard to say
Why there should be such creatures

But once our life gets into them
As sometimes happens
Our poems
Turn into living things
And there's no arguing
With living things
They are
The way they are

Our poems
May be rough
Or delicate
Little
Or great

But always
They have inside them
A confluence of cries
And secret languages

And always
They are improvident
And free
They keep
A kind of Sabbath

They play
On sooty fire escapes
And window ledges

They wander in and out
Of jails and gardens
They sparkle
In the deep mines
They sing
In breaking waves
And rock like wooden cradles.

LOS DESPLAZADOS

Then the old pilgrim found herself alone
Beside a lake of evil
That had no bottom to it,
No further shore.

In the reflections on its burning water
There was a blaze of misery
That blinded human pity,
It was the fifth
Of the five sorrowful mysteries,
It was a civil war,

A village was in flight,
The men, the women fleeing,
The dark-haired children running.
She saw their eyes,
Their eyes.

REFUGEE SERVANT

Twilight has silenced the thrushes
And opened the evening star
The sounds of tennis are over
And now there are voices and laughter
And the rattle of ice in glass

It's time to go down to the kitchen
And Maria stops on the landing
To pin up her black hair
Folding away like a letter
The tin huts and fierce mountains
Of her far native country.

MY ANASTASIA

for Nellie Pysz

1.

My mother ironed all day.
Tomorrow will be Sunday.
How clear, how blue
The jangling air will be!
How starched how snowy white
How rich with bells
The Sabbath clouds will be!
Chimes will be scattered from the rocking bells.
The swallows with their crisp
And joyous wings
Will skim through showers of sound.
The flowers that we gathered
Out in the fields today
Will float above the altar
Buttercup-spangled, light as air
And bright as candles.
We'll have a long procession by the river
And the whole village will turn out for it,
We'll walk that path through the tall grass
Where later we'll be haying.
We'll sing our hymns to Mary as we walk
And from far across the river
We'll hear the singing in the other villages.

2.

My mother died when I was seven
And I tried to cook for my father.
I had a big pot boiling
When he came in from the fields

But I'd only four noodles in it!
Poor child, poor child, my father said.
Both of us cried!
I went straight to the widow next door
And threw my arms around her.
Please marry my father, I said,
He's a good man, he's kind, he doesn't drink,
And she married my father!

3.

When you came to America
Your name was Anastasia
Your humble dignity was in it.
But to the rich who hired you
Your name was unpronounceable,
Your dignity a reproach.
They said We'll have to call you Nellie.

You were only a Polack after all
So they fed you only potatoes.
Is mashed is baked is boiled
You told me,
Is all potatoes!

You and your husband Dominic
Were Democrats at first,
Your bosses were Republicans.
And you said to me
They have the education
They know more
They say Republican is better
So Dominic and I we turned Republican.

When they learned that your birthday
Was the same as George Washington's birthday

They said That can't be true!
It must have been some other day!
But you were born in Poland.
In Poland, you explained to me,
Is no George Washington.

Once on Washington's birthday
We tried to go shopping together,
But the door of the store was locked.
You turned to me and said
Is closed. Is right. Is more respect.
Is father of country.

4.

You and Dominic
Once went to the theater.
In the film a child was born.
The film didn't show the birth,
But you heard the mother groaning
And then the baby's cry.
That wasn't right.
Birth isn't for the theater.
Birth is for home.
You never went again.

When the new big church was built
The old one was up for auction.
Dominic went to watch
But the man standing next to him said
Dominic, bid!
So he bid and his bid was the highest.

He came home to supper
And sat at the supper-table
Pale and not eating

You know how men are
They don't say what's wrong
So you asked him what was wrong
And then he told you,
I bought the church!

Every day after work
You hitched up the wagon
And drove it to the church
For a wagonload of lumber.
Dominic wasn't strong
He couldn't do it.
When you had all the lumber
You put up a house together
And for as long as I knew you
You lived in that house.

5.

I saw you throw a doctor's bill away
Because he hadn't cured you
And if a workman wanted too much money
For too small a job
You were indignant.
Is no more George Washington country!
Is Khrushchev country!

But when the governor divorced
His wife of thirty years
And there was gossip and shock
You only said,
Is weakness.

Though you never hated their children,
For all your life you held a stubborn grudge
Against the Blacks the Yanks the Jews.

This was your one injustice.
In every other way
You mostly were for justice
You always had been poor
Your heart was radical.

6.

When you were old
You wrote Pope Paul in Rome
I'm only a poor old woman
But I love you very much,
And he sent you a printed blessing
Signed with his own hand.
When I saw it, you told me,
I cried three days
I was so happy!
But next time you wrote
A secretary answered.
From now on, he told you,
You may write to me instead.
You were hurt.
You were offended.
Darkly you commented,
Is jealousness!

7.

You were a widow when I knew you
And you had no children
And a priest had told you
Adopt is no good
So you collected clothing
For orphans everywhere,
You answered every appeal.
Your porch was piled with boxes.

You see a picture of a little ragged child
You said to me,
And what else can you do?

Because your brother Joseph who died young
Had been a priest
You loved poor seminarians.
The doctor said, You mustn't take in washing
Any longer.
Still you took in washing
And gave away your earnings
To seminarians and children.

The last time I saw you
You were eighty-four
You were in the hospital
Your hands were tied to the bed.
You'd forgotten English
You'd rejected English.
Please speak to me in English
I begged you,
I don't know any Polish.
But you said Heck with English!
And holding tight to my hand
With your tied-up hand
You spoke to me for a long time in Polish.

8.

In the company of your father
And of your lost mother
With Dominic your husband
And Joseph your brother
And those children you never saw
Who are your children,

No longer hating anyone
You have got back the joy
Of the church bells clanging and tossing
Of the white Sunday dress
Ironed for you by your mother
Of the wildflowers fresh on the altar
And processions along the river

And songs in the open air
Those hymns in honor of Mary
That were the same
In every village
As fieldflowers are the same
In every meadow.

You have got back the joy
And more than all the joy
Of your Polish Sundays.

In the radiant sweetness
And glory of heaven
Pray for me Anastasia
Who was once called Nellie.
In heaven you are called Anastasia.

A TAILOR'S WIFE

I went into the tailor's shop
There was a smell
Of woolly steam
The tailor's little wife
Was there alone
Ironing
A pair of trousers

And there it was in front of me
Astonishing
And unmistakable
That rare element
Alive
In purest silence

In the worn features
Of the tailor's wife
And in her dark
Sicilian eyes.

THE PASTURE ROSE

Rosa humilis
The rose of the pastures
A small peasant rose

Free and for nothing
Gives us her prickles
Her five translucent petals
And her golden eye

And so to thank her
I try to learn
That dialect of silence
Which is her language
And then translate it
Into human words

As if the Lord had told me
Listen to the rose
Be the voice of the rose.

LOVERS

I can still see
The new weather
Diamond-clear
That flowed down from Canada
That day
When the rain was over

I can still see
The main street two blocks long
The weedy edges of the wilderness
Around that sawmill town

And the towering shadows
Of a virgin forest
Along the log-filled river

We walked around
In a small travelling carnival
I can still hear
Its tinny music
And smell its dusty elephants
I can still feel your hand
Holding my hand
That day

When human, quarrelsome
But stronger
Than death or anger
A love began.

NATIVE AMERICANS

Blue eggshells
Empty in the grass,
On the rough-coated hills
Translucent,
The little pasture-rose,

Eagle's shadow
Sweeping the high pasture,
Wordless gospel.

✧　✧　✧

Older than the sun
And younger than the dew,
Poor as the larks
He came into the world

And walked from town to town
Without a stick or sandals
Carrying his new fire.

✧　✧　✧

And today I saw him out on the street
In front of the post office,
Tired out, young,
About the age he was
The day they killed him,

Native pastor
Of a small parish
Up on the Reservation

He stood there listening
To an old Indian woman,
One of his people,

One of his disinherited
And cheated people.

Eagle's shadow
Crossing the high pasture,
Silent gospel.

FOR MY SON JOHNNY

July 11th, 1980

The maker of worlds and tender father of sparrows
Who told us what's done to the smallest is done to him,
Told us also, the least will be greatest in heaven,
And since it was he who told us we know it's true.
So Johnny, now you're one of the greatest,
Because here on earth you were certainly one of the least.

You called yourself "a man without money or power,"
You seemed only to ask to drink countless cans of soda,
Though it did have to be one special brand.
You seemed only to ask
To tell your difficult puns with a delighted smile
To friends and acquaintances and even strangers,
And to stand in front of your house and rock and wave your arms
And sing, varying it with whoops and growls
Of wild ecstatic joy,
And later to inquire of shopkeepers and policemen
If they could hear you at the other end of town.
You seemed to ask only to spend hours in the woods and fields
Alone, "talking to God."

But you also loved to go swimming
Especially in thunderstorms,
Especially in autumn "under the colored leaves"
And if the leaves weren't there you pretended they were there.
You loved napping in the "messy attic
With filing cabinets and old comic books
And empty cartons saying B&M BAKED BEANS."
And passionately you loved the thunder

With all its "fancy sounds"
In which you detected all kinds of subtleties.
"Did it sound like a subway train?
Did it say Relinquish Relinquish?
Did it shake the ground?"

And you loved women, most of whom you admired
Quite regardless of age,
And whom you hugged with great abandon,
Particularly the ones in flowered dresses
And the ones with curly hair,
Knowing you'd never marry because
"A wife might be hard to please."
This may have hurt.
Perhaps that's why you asked to be excused from weddings,
Saying that they were boring.

A little girl once asked you, "Johnny,
How does it feel to be retarded?"
And you answered gently,
"I don't know dear, I'm not retarded."
Which you were not.

Though light-heartedly you described your outbursts of temper
As "just a little jump and a babyish roar,"
Far oftener, your scruples attacked you:
"Am I the worst person in the world?"

Though your shoelaces were hardly ever tied
And you seldom wore matching socks
You tried to behave with dignity in the village
"So as not to embarrass my little sisters."

There was a father in you too somewhere
Though you never corrected other people's children

"I don't want to act like a staff member!"
If you saw a baby in town you'd smile
And with just the tip of one finger
You'd carefully touch the tiny hands and feet.
With the Child in the Christmas manger you did the same.

You told us that "In heaven the angels kid and joke."
Quite casually you'd mention seeing St. Michael the Archangel,
"That's who I just waved to."
We couldn't see him, so we asked what he was like.
You told us, "Just a friendly man in a business suit,"
And said "Next time I see an Archangel
Would it be all right to ask him his name?"

Often you visited our parish church,
First splashing on much holy water.
Inside the church you went down hard on both knees
And then, dropping a lot of flaming matches,
You lighted almost a full row of candles
To pray for "blind and deaf and crippled children."

"And when the church is locked," you said,
"I just go up to it and touch the wall."

Your family sent you away to live on a farm in Vermont,
And for years your times at home were so short and so far apart
That hearing them once called "visits" you turned white,
So deep was your speechless fear
That you might be only a guest at home, and have no home.
But in your humility you knew how to forgive,
Growing kinder and kinder as you grew older.

"I'm not afraid of dying," you said, "just of getting hurt."
Johnny, now you're a staff member!

And now you're home.
Now you're with Mary, whose starry veil you loved,
And of whom you said, "She won't get bored with my puns,"
And, "She won't mind if I touch her dress."
While your mother, who sometimes did get bored with your puns,
Cries here on earth

And asks you, now that you're one of the greatest,
To grant her a portion of your littleness.

THÉRÈSE

Thérèse, your statue's in our parish church,
But when you were a child you crossed these mountains
And drank the clear rock-shattered mountain water
And picked the daisies in the soaring meadows

And crept like us, over the black ravines.
"I can fall only into God," you said.

There was a church in Umbria, Little Portion,
Already old eight hundred years ago.
It was abandoned and in disrepair
But it was called St. Mary of the Angels
For it was known to be the haunt of angels,
Often at night the country people
Could hear them singing there.

What was it like, to listen to the angels,
To hear those mountain-fresh, those simple voices
Poured out on the bare stones of Little Portion
In hymns of joy?
No one has told us.
Perhaps it needs another language
That we have still to learn,
An altogether different language.

FOR JOSHUA, ONE MONTH OLD

Joshua, your hands and fingers
Are so light and small
That when you fall asleep
You rest them on the air.
Gravity has no hold on them
And has to leave them there.

A CHILD AT THE CIRCUS

When you're a traveller and the evening air turns golden
Every house you pass begins to look like home
Because it's supper-time, it's time to be at home.
But there's another stormier light that's golden-green
With the chemical green beauty of green beans cooked in soda
Or the false gold light on the false green trees of the theater.

When I see this kind of light I remember being a small child
    at the theater
When the curtain came up on a banquet of wonder and belief.
Scene One: A Wood.
The princess came on stage with her waist-length hair
And the regal flash of her sequins broke into the play
Like taxi-horns in the street when they clash with a concert.
I believed that the princess was a princess in real life,
Everything was real life.
I had no unbelief,
Everything was equally believable because nothing made sense,
The entire world was one big surprise,
Even a shock.
Whether it was the man in the play who had a donkey head
Or the raisin-spotted pudding at my grandmother's, when it burst
    into flames
And I dove under the table,
Or that morning when there was white stuff all over the grass
And I asked if it was sugar and my big sisters laughed,
Whether it was the leaves of the columbine turning to silver
    under water
As my mother showed me,
Or the black and orange turtle who hissed at me in the
    strawberry-patch,

Or the sparrow singing beet greens, beet greens as if he could talk
    like us,
Or the wet bloody kittens coming out of my cat's belly,
It was all brand-new and none of it made sense
And I didn't expect it to make sense.

The circus was like the rest of the world, only more so.
It was always our grandfather who took us there.
Since he was a doctor, which is a grown-up of grown-ups,
And even a psychiatrist on top of that,
He had to do without a certain kind of wonder,
But he wanted to give it to us.

In the circus were all the colors of the rainbow,
There was glitter and whirling and jumping and coarse music,
There were shuffling, swaying elephants, rippling their skins,
Shifting from foot to foot,
Always in motion like the sea.
There was a dancing pony with chalk-white wings
That I believed were real
Until my grandfather said they were artificial.
That was a grown-up's word, but I knew he was saying
There's something not quite right about wings on a pony.
It was a bit disappointing.

The entertainment I liked the best of all
Was to sit out on the back steps with my brother
Enjoying the company of our grandfather's coachman
Michael Grady
And his rich rolling stories.
He sat between us,
And while he was telling the stories I peered at his greenish eyes
In which there were little brown threads as wonderful
    as the stories.

A SHORT TESTAMENT

Whatever harm I may have done
In all my life in all your wide creation
If I cannot repair it
I beg you to repair it,

And then there are all the wounded
The poor the deaf the lonely and the old
Whom I have roughly dismissed
As if I were not one of them.
Where I have wronged them by it
And cannot make amends
I ask you
To comfort them to overflowing,

And where there are lives I may have withered around me,
Or lives of strangers far or near
That I've destroyed in blind complicity,
And if I cannot find them
Or have no way to serve them,

Remember them. I beg you to remember them

When winter is over
And all your unimaginable promises
Burst into song on death's bare branches.

WARTIME SUNDAY

In honor of Eugene Atget, photographer of Paris

From the time of a long-ago war that destroyed only
    far-away cities
I remember a Sunday walk with the littlest of our sons.
The vomit of Saturday night was wet in the doorways,
No one was up, First Avenue empty and gray,
So we turned a corner to stare at the three bridges,
Great webs of stillness over the East River.

On our way home, passing the locked-up shops
We saw one window heaped with tarnished lamps
Guitars and radios and dusty furs
And there among them a pawned christening-dress
White as a waterfall.

FROM DENVER TO ALBUQUERQUE

Green is water's bride, we see them always together
Along gold-bearing creeks in these high western mountains
Waves of rock surge above us to bare inaccessible heights
Stained with their lofty grape-blue shadows,
While bluebells, coral-bells and wild white poppies
Bloom fearless on the ledges.

Next we look down into a small ravine
Brimmed with eddying swallows
And pass a few wire crosses twined with plastic flowers
Set in a mountain graveyard under tawny cliffs.
We come out over a valley dense with trailers
Where suddenly the showers fuse with sunlight
And a frail rainbow shines.

Then we stop at a gas-pump in an adobe town
Where the young men are drinking beer and talking
Around a broken car.
On the grimy wall of the washroom someone has printed:
LOVE IS AMONG US,

And here an Indian climbs into the bus.
He's blind, his eyes are white,
And with him there's a woman, sister, mistress, wife,
They alone know.
They share the meal they brought with them
And fall asleep in one another's arms.

As we cross the Rockies and the Sangre de Cristo mountains
Wary or drugged or sleeping,
To each of us in our sprawling disarray,
Out of the stabbed heart of the mountain-maker
A freshet pours.

A YEAR OF JUBILEE

You grew up like a sapling
With fishermen and shepherds
And the God-haunted mountains
Of your small holy country

You looked the same
As all your people
So for a time
You went unnoticed
You who were later killed
Most cruelly

One Sabbath morning
You stood up in the temple
Young village rabbi
From the provinces

And you unrolled the scroll
And read aloud from it
The Word welled up to us
Out of Isaiah's book
As fresh as the clear streams
That well up in the mountains

"The spirit of the Lord
Has come upon me
He has anointed me
To bring glad tidings
To the poor
To heal the brokenhearted
To give the blind their sight
To free the captives

Release the prisoners and proclaim
A year of jubilee"

We recognized the voice
This was the Promised One
This was the Shepherd
Our hearts were burning.

We listened when you told us
About our heavenly Father
Who wishes us
To cherish one another
To be forgiving, generous
As he is himself

And festive, carefree
As the meadow-flowers
Light as the swallows

He wishes us
To be like children

You also told us
Our Father
Blesses us most of all
When we are poor

So even when our bodies
Have grown old
And our heads are filled with confusion

He will not love us
Any the less for that.

A NIGHT IN IRELAND

Our steamship docked at night
In Cobh, an Irish seaport
A small one in those days

Not an inn, not a tavern was open
And we had to wait till morning
For the train to Fermoy

But in the wooded hills
Up above the town
Nightingales were awake
All the dark thickets
Were rich with their songs

It was on that night
And in those woods
I dreamed that I found the door
Of all doors the most hidden
And most renowned

Overgrown with nettles
Rustic and low
Built as if for children
Or as a gate for sheep
In some back-country pasture

And through a chink in the door
I saw the marvelous light
That's purest of all lights
Neither sun nor moon
Nor any star I know of
Could give such light

And I saw the crowds of the blessed
From the greatest to the smallest
The smallest were running and laughing
And Christ the Lord was with them
And also Mary

But before I could knock at the door
Someone spoke to me
I think it was an angel

He said You've come too soon
Go back into the towns
Live there as love's apprentice
And God will give you his kingdom

I woke up just before sunrise
When the nightingales ended their songs
Dew gathered on the ferns
And the cool woods
Gave off a scent of earth
In the early morning

I was hungry and cold
And I started back to the town
At the first signs of day

Already a sunlit smoke
Was rising from the chimneys
And mist from the water

I heard a rooster crowing
And then I heard the whistle
Of the train to Fermoy.

ON THE THREE-HOUR TRAIN RIDE

First we pass a farm
And see dark wings flare up
Out of a patch of grain

We see the water-loving willows
With their slim leaves
And the tall rushes in the swamp
Their fleeces filled with light

Here's a wide inlet
Perfectly still
Glazed with the tender colors
Of the morning sky

And here's a fisherman
With his rod and creel
Standing alone
Thigh-deep in water

His spirit
Will outlast the earth

And here's an acre of crushed cars
And there's a refuse heap
That's white with seagulls

Here blindfolded with boards
Is an abandoned factory
In a field of yarrow

Here closer to the city
Some small pleasure boats

Dance at their moorings
In the dirty river

King David says
We're thirsty

For God
For the living God

When will we see His face?

SOUTHWESTERN MOUNTAINS

The plane is sinking by stages,
Its long descent has started,
Slanting towards Albuquerque,
Quaking on wide stiff wings.
Fathoms beneath us
In the night-black folds of the mountains
Secret and wild
The Indian villages sparkle.

Morning will show me the mountains
Huge in their cloaks of stone,
Carved with deep watercourses.
The sun has taken the water
But a rough growth follows the streambeds
And all the foothills are dotted
With those low spicy bushes
That are firewood and incense in one.

Then there are cone-shaped mountains
Standing around like strangers.
Even in broad daylight
They are as red as sunrise,
Nothing like the others.

Out of the prickly desert,
In the midst of its perfect flatness
There flies up single and sheer
A towering sudden rock
Sacred to the Indians,
Who called it the Wingéd Stone.
A citadel for swallows
It serves no human purposes
Except the purpose of wonder.

Spellbound by the heat
The desert creatures are hiding.
Only their caretaker
The prairie owl
Regards us, small beside his burrow,
His wilderness wrapped around him.

The mountains in blue distance
Are floating lightly as a song.
Far to the east and north
Old men and women
Are laboring up the stairs
Of their dark tenements,
And further still
In the streets of the coastal cities
Children are chanting
Their skip-rope rhymes.

FOUR POEMS IN ONE

At six o'clock this morning
I saw the rising sun
Resting on the ground like a boulder
In the thicket back of the school,
A single great ember
About the height of a man.

✧   ✧   ✧

Night has gone like a sickness,
The sky is pure and whole.
Our Lady of Poland spire
Is rosy with first light,
Starlings above it shatter their dark flock.
Notes of the Angelus
Leave their great iron cup
And slowly, three by three
Visit the Polish gardens round about,
Dahlias shaggy with frost
Sheds with their leaning tools
Rosebushes wrapped in burlap
Skiffs upside down on trestles
Like dishes after supper.

✧   ✧   ✧

These are the poems I'd show you
But you're no longer alive.
The cables creaked and shook
Lowering the heavy box.
The rented artificial grass
Still left exposed

That gritty gash of earth
Yellow and mixed with stones
Taking your body
That never in this world
Will we see again, or touch.

✧ ✧ ✧

We know little
We can tell less
But one thing I know
One thing I can tell
I will see you again in Jerusalem
Which is of such beauty
No matter what country you come from
You will be more at home there
Than ever with father or mother
Than even with lover or friend
And once we're within her borders
Death will hunt us in vain.

THE NEIGHBORING SEA

At three in the morning the village is all in silence
But the silence is afloat on the roar of the sea
And all the streets are bathed in the roar of the sea
The waves are at their labors
Cresting and flooding all along the shore
Tumbling and spinning the kelp and the devils-apron
Threshing to meal the morsels and crumbs of stone
And the light seashells with their storm-blue linings.

This is the time of day when I remember
That down at the end of the street there is an ocean
A Nation of fishes and whales
A sky-colored country stretching from here to Spain
A liquid kingdom dragged about by the moon.

ON THE MAINE ISLANDS

No one will see
The light-stepping deer
When they come out from the alders
To look for windfalls
In the abandoned orchard.

No one will see the daylilies
The color of red foxes,
Waist-high coarse-textured lilies
That spring from the tumbled stones
Where there was once a farmhouse
And crowd around the cellar-hole
Now thick with raspberry-canes
Where hornets forage.

Mink live here, and voles,
There are seals on the offshore ledges
And herons with their harsh cries
Are nesting up in the woods,
But the man who was down by the shore
Scraping the hull of a boat
The woman feeding her hens
The child playing with fir-cones
Have been gone for a hundred years
And in the still harbor
There's no skiff but ours.

     ✧   ✧   ✧

These granite and limestone islands,
These tops of flooded mountains
Are scattered all over the bay

Their clearings shining with wildflowers,
The live coals of hawkweed,
The daisies' fiery white,
And finespun birdsongs shiver
Over their scraps of forest.

They're moated with ice-cold channels
Deep enough for a whale,
Where once or twice a summer
With a slow throb of engines
The Swedish freighters go by.

When the sun comes out
The sky speaks blue
And the whole bay
Down to its least cove
Takes on a dazzle of blue,
Becomes a field of splendor.

✧   ✧   ✧

High up over the harbor
Of the fishing village
On another island
Is St. Mary Star of the Sea,
Built by Italian stonecutters
Who came to work in the quarries
It's a white frame building
The size of a one-room schoolhouse,
With six milky windows
And a low spire.
Below are the steep-pitched streets
And the fishermen's wooden houses
With their stacks of lobster pots
Their granite garden walls
And their small gardens flaming
In the short northern summer.

Through St. Mary's windows
Half open in the summer
We can see the harbor,
The water bluer than larkspur,
The sloping folds of granite.

An old Italian woman
Who gets to Mass early
Has come with dahlias and roses,
And the stonecutters' grandchildren
Carefully chant the Gloria
In their transparent voices

For the one who carved the islands
Has come to live among us,
And this is the house he has chosen,
St. Mary Star of the Sea.

IN STORM-WATCH SEASON

The foaming clematis
Has finished blooming
The autumn
Equinox is here
The air is very still
But day and night
Storms in the Caribbean
Keep the Atlantic roaring

The ocean
Is pouring fog
Into the trees
And with it the fresh smells
Of eelgrass and of kelp
Float inland from the torn
And churning beaches

In the storm-haunted evening
A cricket
Has begun to sing
A streetlamp shines
Deep in the fog
A burr
Of golden light

In three months' time
We will have snow
In three months' time
The savior will be born.

SONG FOR THE TOWN OF ASSISI

"Why is this little city
Not like any other
Not like any other?"
—OLD SPANISH CAROL

Holy and steep
And radiant Assisi
I know now
That on this side of Paradise
I'll never visit you
I'll never make that journey
I'll never see you
Except in pictures

I'll never hear your bells
Or see your cobbled streets
The walls that Giotto painted
Or the houses of Francis and Clare
I never will look down
On the Spoleto valley
Your deep plunging valley
That's beautiful even in pictures

And you, Francis' tunic
Reproach and treasure
Brown homespun tunic
Patched all over
I'll never see you
Except in pictures

And I know now
I'll never climb
That high wooded mountain
Where Francis had his cave

On one September night
Beside that very cave
The five wounds of the Passion
Pierced him through and through

And even now
His every wound is singing

I wonder
What birds are nesting
On Mount Alverna now
What flowers are growing there
What kinds of trees

Hill town
Ancient town
Town
Where I'm a foreigner

Small city
Walled city
Unlike any other

My chosen city

Festive Assisi
Reproach and treasure
Hoarding nothing
Storing up nothing

You welcome lepers
And dine with them
And where your shadow falls
The wolf grows gentle

How long
Must I live far away from you
Both outwardly and inwardly
So far away

I've never even learned
Your language

And I know now
I'll never see you
Never visit you
This side of the Jordan
The river Jordan

But I will surely find you
On the other side of the river
Francis blind and bleeding
Francis bleeding and singing
Will have translated you
To the other side of the river
Cobble by cobble
Stone by stone

And I will find you there
I'll surely find you there
Holy and steep
And radiant Assisi
I'll surely find you there

Free of all coveting
Festive Assisi
Where lepers are welcome
Where the poor are honored

Where the wolf grows gentle
I know I'll surely find you

Beyond the river
Beyond the Jordan river
Beyond the black the terrible
The blessed river.

FARMYARD BY MOONLIGHT

There must be a farmer asleep here under the eaves
Filling his room with the surf-like sound of his breathing
As he takes deep draughts of rest
Gathering all of it in before the morning.
His large weathered hands have fallen open
And in a patch of moonlight on the floor
His heavy wooden shoes are resting too.

Below the torn bright edges of a thatch of cloud
A small moon watches, who has been appointed
To guard this human sleep.
She offers her colorless radiance
To the dark clumsy beast-like presences
Of the stone farmhouse and the thick stone walls
And sheds her light
Over the lean-to and the ladder,
Over a wheelbarrow spilling its bunch of sticks,
A thin black sheepdog mysteriously awake
A glint of water left by the last rain
And a slatted gate that answers her with its shadow.

Walt Whitman honored you, Jean-François Millet,
He said you could read the gospel of the earth.
And I thank you myself
For giving me what no one else could give me,
This farm that in Norman Gruchy a hundred years ago
Lay hushed under the moon.
You saved it for us out of that warm life
Which God has hidden somewhere,
And out of your hands and eyes which now are dust.

IN CHARTRES

Through fields of ripe wheat
In France, in the heart of France
We've come on foot from Paris
To these incredible stones
To this tidal wave of the Sabbath
Rising up out of the wheat
With its village gathered around it
To its portals crowded with prophets
With patriarchs and with martyrs
Tall in the long folds
Of their carven robes.

This one is Abraham
With one hand he's holding the knife
The knife of sacrifice
And with his other hand
He's tenderly cupping the cheek
Of Isaac, his little son
There's a look of calm wonder
On the face of his little son
Whose feet are already bound
And under his feet is the ram
The ram who will take his place
As the victim of sacrifice.

Abraham, it's you especially
Whom I have come to see
You are our father in faith
In this knapsack on my back
I'm bringing you all the deaths
That I can't understand
And not the deaths alone

But also the pain
The deaths from all the famines
From holocaust and war
And every unjust death
Of the innocent and the humble.

To take the place of the child
Isaac there was a ram
But for all of those others
There was no ram
And I lay down all these deaths
I lay them down at your feet
So that you can keep them for me
Since by myself
I am unable
To understand them.

✧　✧　✧

Inside the portal a young
Girl from a nearby farm, a girl
Slight as a minnow
Tugs at the heavy bell-rope
To sound the Angelus
She has to lift her bare feet off
The flagstones, and throw her head
Way back, her long brown braids
Are swinging backwards
And high above her
In the belfry shaggy with tiles
The ancient bell obeys her
The pigeons that live in the towers
Wheel up into the sky
The air rocks and trembles
And the slow notes of the bell
Open into the sky

Till they lose themselves in the air
And sink down into the wheat
Among the poppies and cornflowers
Beside the skylark's nest.

✧ ✧ ✧

Once long ago
In the French countryside
In the province of Oise

I came on a little church
That for some reason
Was deep in the fields
And away from the village

It had a statue of Mary
Like something made by a child
And on Mary's altar
In a jar of water
There was a bunch of daisies
Which someone must have gathered
That same morning

And in the rough shell
Of the whitewashed nave
There was a stone coolness

And the faint bitter smell
Of the rural
Churches of France

It could be the scent of hops
Or some hidden yeast or lichen
But I don't know

It's the scent of a secret world
A secret of the fields
It's here too in the porches
Of Our Lady of Chartres.

✧   ✧   ✧

We've come through the leather doors
We've entered the forest of praise
There in the high half darkness
We see its constellations
We see the glowing embers
Of a dark fire
We see the lancet windows
And the great North Rose
Whose blue is blue
As blood is red
Whose red is radiant

Father you have allowed us
For once you have permitted us
To make a thing so beautiful
As to be no less beautiful
Than your own Creation.

A LIST OF PRAISES

Give praise with psalms that tell the trees to sing,
Give praise with Gospel choirs in storefront churches,
Mad with the joy of the Sabbath,
Give praise with the babble of infants, who wake with the sun,
Give praise with children chanting their skip-rope rhymes,
A poetry not in books, a vagrant mischievous poetry
Living wild on the streets through generations of children.

Give praise with the sound of the milk-train far away
With its mutter of wheels and long-drawn-out sweet whistle
As it speeds through the fields of sleep at three in the morning,
Give praise with the immense and peaceful sigh
Of the wind in the pinewoods,
At night give praise with starry silences.

Give praise with the skirling of seagulls
And the rattle and flap of sails
And gongs of buoys rocked by the sea-swell
Out in the shipping-lanes beyond the harbor.
Give praise with the humpback whales,
Huge in the ocean they sing to one another.

Give praise with the rasp and sizzle of crickets, katydids and
      cicadas,
Give praise with hum of bees,
Give praise with the little peepers who live near water.
When they fill the marsh with a shimmer of bell-like cries
We know that the winter is over.

Give praise with mockingbirds, day's nightingales.
Hour by hour they sing in the crepe myrtle
And glossy tulip trees
On quiet side streets in the southern towns.

Give praise with the rippling speech
Of the eider-duck and her ducklings
As they paddle their way downstream
In the red-gold morning
On Restiguche, their cold river,
Salmon river,
Wilderness river.

Give praise with the whitethroat sparrow.
Far, far from the cities,
Far even from the towns,
With piercing innocence
He sings in the spruce-tree tops,
Always four notes
And four notes only.

Give praise with water,
With storms of rain and thunder
And the small rains that sparkle as they dry,
And the faint floating ocean roar
That fills the seaside villages,
And the clear brooks that travel down the mountains

And with this poem, a leaf on the vast flood,
And with the angels in that other country.

FOUR SEASONS CAROL

The barbs of cruel Auschwitz
Grow back again and again
Hiroshima's poison
Gluts the arsenals
While tyranny and famine
Are withering Africa.

Our coldness greed and war
Multiply past counting
The deaths of children
And the wounds of the poor

Whose bitter wants and sorrows
Are splinters of your Passion
Jesus, hunted Child.

Then grant us grace to bring them
More than stale crusts and empty prayers
That hinder your just kingdom.

HERE ON EARTH

The old man living
In his rented room
Grows lonely as the night comes on
Especially in winter

And the boy shooting drugs
On the tenement roof
Is lonely whether or not
He has companions

Lovers lie sleeping
Side by side
A wilderness between them

And their unborn infant
Is already alone
So soon to be discarded
Even as he begins
Unfolding in the womb
Of his lonely mother

Because the scatterer
Has overtaken us
Betraying promises
Estranging lovers

Tearing us inwardly
And tearing us apart
One from another

And this is why
Those of us who are sated

Find it so easy to ignore
Those of us who are starving

And why we have been known
To torture one another
Why there are times
When we are far more cruel
Than the animals.

Nevertheless
Taken all together
Or taken one by one
We are the holiest
Of all earth's creatures

For he who kindled
The fire of the sun
He who draws out the tender leaves
From the dark twigs of winter

He who has whittled
A cabin for the snail
Has also carved our names
In the palm of his hand

And he became a child
The better to be near us
Born in the wintertime
Born on a journey

He grew to be a man
And lived among us
To be our healing
When we were sick
Our bread
When we were hungry

To be the wine
At all our weddings

He suffered at our hands
And he forgave us
He sweat from head to foot
With human anguish
And shedding every drop of blood
To give us to each other

He gave himself to us
That we might live forever

He gave us even more
Than he has given the angels.

A DEPOSITION

The nursemaid Agnes Cassidy
A woman not much bigger
Than a child
The eldest of thirteen

Came straight from Donegal

One of her eyes
Was pulled askew
Mauled by the forceps
Of a country doctor
Who had been drinking
The night that she was born

But her small flat
Unlucky face
Bore marks
Of Celtic beauty

And she was strong

Her faith was silent
Sure
And passionate

She'd gladly walk
Ten miles
In any weather
For a taste of God

And when her mother died
In Ireland

And a fierce sense of duty
Was dragging her
Back to the farm in Donegal
To help her father

She wept at leaving
The little fiery boy
Whose nurse she'd been

Whom she had named
The Fighting Irishman

And whom she loved she said
As much as she loved anyone.

THE WEIHNACHTS-HISTORIE

When you wrote the *Weihnachts-Historie,* Heinrich Schütz, you
    were near eighty.
You struck the gnarled root of Jesse
And from it sprang this intricate grove of music
Weaving a cage where the brightest nova that ever burned
    in the sky
Sings like a thrush, sings for a poor child.
You swaddle and cradle the child in madrigals
And taking a psalm you twist him a royal crown.
You summon for him a river of angels that pour their voices
Into his broken shelter like sparks, or abundant grain.
From around a fire of sticks in a frozen pasture
You fetch him the bleating of whittled flutes, and the first
    hoarse carols.
Then out of this brambly, soaring and tangling triumph, strong
As the holiest stones of Europe,
A single voice shakes itself free,
The Aramaic lullaby
Floating light and alone down the Egyptian brook,
The shallow seasonal brook that travellers drink.
He has begun to travel with us. He tastes the brackish
Lukewarm water,
And is jarred by the humps in the stony road.

THE SHORTEST DAYS

Hold out your hands, God my Father,
Because I want to give you my old age,
Or at least, try to give you my old age

Beginning with the dusk of this morning in Advent.
In the small frame houses round the station
Honey-colored light fills up the kitchens
Where old handymen and widows, pensioners and spinsters
Are boiling water for the day's first coffee or tea
While the tiny maple-leaves are curling like birds' feet round
     the frost,
Through all the whispering to you in buses
As I ride to see grandchildren
Or to greet the eighty-year-old heart breaking in a hospital bed,
The hands that served you strapped to the rails of the bed,
(And may that heart be broken into your hands.)

Through all your lights, sparkling glowing glittering
     flashing blazing,
And truth, your terrible light,
Through fears for my old husband and grown children, and joys
     when they have joy,
Through "clouds, calms and all weathers,"
Through all the unknown history through the unknown sicknesses
     through the unknown death.

God my Father, hold out your hands
So I may place in them this promissory note, this title-deed,
This poem, here on this page.

DECEMBER

Out in the middle of the lake
Some men who work for the village
Have moored
A floating Christmas tree

At night I see it
From my bedroom window
It rocks a little
Drifts a little
In the wind from the ocean
A fiery cone of jewels.

CAUSE OF OUR JOY

Rock crystal
Clearer than crystal
Stronger than rock

Snow crown of Sinai
Melting on the heights
Pouring through the valleys
In pure rushing water
And wine that sings of justice.

    ✧   ✧   ✧

Chosen from the chosen
Mystical rose
Your creature petals
Mirror that beauty
No one can see and live
You hide in your heart
Like dew simple and silent
That blazing majesty.

Small as you are, your fragrance
Fills all the world,
Fragrance of hope,
Fragrance of the gospels.

Come to the old woman
Whose lodging is the street
Come to the drugged boy
The landlord, the general
Come to the hunted hunter by his jungle river
Come to the banker, the prisoner, the torturer

The hungry, the shut-in, the runaway in danger
Come to the backward child.

Whether or not we know you
Come to rich and poor
Come to us all.

✧　✧　✧

Star of morning
There is still such darkness
Only by the light
Of your innocent fire
We know this is the morning.

But sweet in this dark morning
Is a freshness of new bread
And the newborn Word in his cradle
Is just beginning to stir.

Queen of Angels
You're up early
Washing, baking, sweeping,
Young country girl
From a scorned province

Broken for the broken

Wife of a carpenter
Mother of a convict
Cause of our joy.

LA BELLA NOTIZIA

a Nativity for my friends

We're at the winter solstice
With its long nights
Wars are still not over
Weapons are heaped on weapons
Terror is hoarded like grain
Those who have no houses
Are sleeping out in the street
Scorched by the burning cold
And children are learning to starve
Before they learn to speak

But this December night
Is like no other night
Angels blaze in the pasture
And all the sheep are kneeling
The brambles have thrown open
Their sweet-smelling flowers
While somewhere back in the hills
All the cocks are crowing
And there are brooks of torchlight
Streaming down the hillside
Where the shepherds are

I'll try to catch up with the shepherds
As they go out searching
For that holy Child
Who's offering us his peace

Who out of love for us
Has chosen to be born

Of a young poor woman
In a cattle shed

Where swaddled in strips
Of a torn shirt
Just as the angel told us
He shines in the dark valley.

ST. JOHN'S DAY

Christmas is two days past
And it's the feast of John
In the dusky twilight
Of the winter morning
Our breath shows white

There's a leftover moon
Hoarfrost on the grass
Light in a kitchen window
And a cat running home
As if she were night itself
Quickly she slips away
Under the hedges

In the small wooden church
Near the railroad station
Mass is beginning
For the old women
Of the neighborhood
Who come here every day
In flowered shawls
Or knitted caps
With canes beside them

The vigil candles
Have all been lighted
And shine like rubies
The fir-trees by the altar
Are still on fire with Christmas
A plaster shepherd-boy
In a blue smock
Still plays a silent flute

Beside the Manger.
The Christ-Child much too big
Holds out his arms

God has become a child
His heart is beating
Only keep very quiet
And you can hear it.

A FOREST PILGRIMAGE

A winter storm has come up in the forest
And we're on pilgrimage
To the shrine of Our Lady of Woodcutters,
Built in the forest by the charcoal-burners
Who were living here two hundred years ago.

And here it is, Our Lady of Woodcutters,
A wooden chapel in a stand of pine.
Wind and sleet pour in as we open the door,
The flame that's burning in a ruby cup
Leaps like a wild thing trying to get free.
The freshness of the wilderness is here
And scent of pine,
The little shrine is brimmed with solitude
Up to its gilded rafters.

And here is the icon that came from Novgorod,
All caked with pearls as an anchor is coated with barnacles
When it has lain in the sea for a long time.
In two places the pearls have been scraped away
Like frost from a windowpane,
To show us the olive-dark face of the Mother of God
And the wise dusky face of her infant Son.
From the crust of jewels they look at us with love.

We don't know how we're going to get home,
Our path on the satiny pine needles of the forest floor
Lies hidden under the snow.
But looking into the eyes of the Mother of God,
Her somewhat sorrowful eyes,
All at once we notice, tiny against her throat,
The Child's lifted fingers blessing the whole world.

CHRISTMAS IN CRAKOW

Cats and their kittens lead their velvet lives
Under the bridges of the Vistula
River of ice and more than a hundred swans
The riverbank is thronged with children
Coasting on makeshift sleds in the deep snow
Above them shine the freshly gilded spires
Of the ancient castle.

This is a cherished city
It has no laws against beauty
Brocade covers the walls of even the smallest café
Doors in the darkest alleys are carved with animals and flowers
And there are people here who smile at strangers.

Above the square on a balcony silver with ice
A choir of schoolchildren is caroling
"The Lord was born for us today
In straw, in hay
The Lord was born for us today
Of the Virgin Mary

In straw the Lord was born for us

On wood, on wood he died for us
From earth, from earth he rose for us
In Bread, in Bread he dwells with us
We sing, we sing for joy!"

WINTER TWILIGHT

On a clear winter's evening
The crescent moon

And the round squirrels' nest
In the bare oak

Are equal planets.

IN CHILDHOOD

The first time
I saw the morning star
I was a small child
Two years old or three
I woke up sobbing

My mother came to me
Gathered me in her arms
And took me to the window
Look she said
There's the morning star

I soon gave over crying
For there it was alone
In the dawn sky
Bright and very beautiful
As beautiful as my mother.

GETTING UP EARLY

Just as the night was fading
Into the dusk of morning
When the air was cool as water
When the town was quiet
And I could hear the sea

I caught sight of the moon
No higher than the rooftops
Our neighbor the moon

An hour before the sunrise
She glowed with her own sunrise
Gold in the grey of morning

World without town or forest
Without wars or sorrows
She paused between two trees

And it was as if in secret
Not wanting to be seen
She chose to visit us
So early in the morning.

LEAVETAKING

Nearing the start of that mysterious last season
Which brings us to the close of the other four,
I'm somewhat afraid and don't know how to prepare
So I will praise you.

I will praise you for the glaze on buttercups
And for the pearly scent of wild fresh water
And the great crossbow shapes of swans flying over
With that strong silken threshing sound of wings
Which you gave them when you made them without voices.

And I will praise you for crickets.
On starry autumn nights
When the earth is cooling
Their rusty diminutive music
Repeated over and over
Is the very marrow of peace.

And I praise you for crows calling from treetops
The speech of my first village,
And for the sparrow's flash of song
Flinging me in an instant
The joy of a child who woke
Each morning to the freedom
Of her mother's unclouded love
And lived in it like a country.

And I praise you that from vacant lots
From only broken glass and candy wrappers
You raise up the blue chicory flowers.

I thank you for that secret praise
Which burns in every creature,
And I ask you to bring us to life
Out of every sort of death

And teach us mercy.

SEPTEMBER-WEED

Because it blooms exactly at the time
When grapes are ripe for wine
In France this small white aster
Is called the Vintager

And now from every casual patch of weeds
And all along the road's rough borders
Its thronging delicate
Dusty constellations
Cry out to us that he is close at hand
Who lets himself be gathered
To be our wine and bread
Mixing our fearful sorrows with his own
Till they are happiness.

LOOKING AT THE SKY

I never will have time
I never will have time enough
To say
How beautiful it is
The way the moon
Floats in the air
As easily
And lightly as a bird
Although she is a world
Made all of stone.

I never will have time enough
To praise
The way the stars
Hang glittering in the dark
Of steepest heaven
Their dewy sparks
Their brimming drops of light
So fresh so clear
That when you look at them
It quenches thirst.

A NOVEMBER SUNRISE

Wild geese are flocking and calling in pure golden air,
Glory like that which painters long ago
Spread as a background for some little hermit
Beside his cave, giving his cloak away,
Or for some martyr stretching out
On her expected rack.
A few black cedars grow nearby
And there's a donkey grazing.

Small craftsmen, steeped in anonymity like bees,
Gilded their wooden panels, leaving fame to chance,
Like the maker of this wing-flooded golden sky,
Who forgives all our ignorance
Both of his nature and of his very name,
Freely accepting our one heedless glance.

BEFORE THE FROST

These are the nights
When every cricket sings
When in the dark around us
There is a flowering
Jubilant continuous
Festival of crickets

They sing together all night long
Drawing a pulsing
Chiming joy
Out of the dryness
Of their tiny bodies

The sky
Is black and clear tonight
The stars in their mountain villages
Glitter in silence

But in the trilling crickets
Among the autumn grasses
The stars
Have found their voices.

RED SKY AT NIGHT

At about five o'clock in the evening on the 7th of December
There was at first an ordinary sunset,
But after sundown there bled into the sky
Such an immense flood of dusky red-gold fire
That every house, barn, shed, tree, twig and blade of grass
And every worker bound for home
Was drenched in it and glowing.
Even when night had fallen
There lingered a long band of smoldering dark glory
Over the far horizon hedged with soot-black trees.

They say it was something like that on one September night
When the six-winged Seraph
Printed the little poor man with the wounds of Christ.
The sky was set aflame over Mount Alverna
Shining into the windows of the inns
For miles around
So that the muleteers woke and saddled and loaded their beasts
And thinking day was breaking
Continued on their journey towards Romagna.
Only when they had gone some distance did the night come back,
And after that, they saw the real sun rising.

FIRE, AND TORRENTIAL RAIN

It's midnight, I'm alone
My house is suddenly sheathed
In a thick tent of rain
These sheaves of throbbing water
This quenching cold
This dark poured into dark
Are the pure opposite
Of fire, and yet this night
Is whispering and singing like a fire.

✧   ✧   ✧

Fire, most beautiful of flowers,
Whose only perfume is brightness,
You have no season, and you bloom
On the highest of high altars
And under the vagrant's pot.
Through centuries on centuries
Like Christ you are everywhere,
To kindle the half cigarettes
Which the homeless find in the gutters,
And the tall paschal candle.

AN EASTER LILY

Tonight the sky received
A paschal moon
It came on time
And through half-open shutters
Its ceremonial radiance
Enters our houses

I for my part received
An Easter lily
Whose whiteness
Is past belief

Its blossoms
The shape of trumpets
Are mute as swans

But deep and strong as sweat
Is their feral perfume.

AT THE SHORE

A slow Atlantic spring
A lingering coolness
Trees quenched and stripped
As if for winter
The leafless bushes grey
Or brown as animals

Bu here and there
I see a field
That's newly plowed
Or one that's fresh and green

And under bramble thickets
The early daffodils
That have escaped from gardens
Are lighting their small fires.

OAKS AND SQUIRRELS

Genesis 18:27

"I speak to my Lord though I am dust and ashes,"
A handful of ashes the wind will soon send flying
Into the drifted oak-leaves under the hedge.
No gardener ever rakes there
Only the squirrels gather bedding there
When they stack up their rustling nests.

You have granted me more time
On earth than the squirrels, less time than the oak,
Whose secret takes a hundred years to tell.
Out of the acorn in the dirt
Its wooden sticks come up
Already knowing how to grow their leaves
And when to spend them all,
Knowing exactly
How to thread up into a winter sky
A dark-veined map like that of a great river
Spun out in tapering streams,
Twig by twig ascending and unfolding
Until at night its topmost buds
Enter the country of the stars.

By day
The squirrels run like script along its boughs
And write their lives with their light bodies.
They are afraid of us
We can never hold them
And there's no room for us in their invisible ark,
Our home is warring disobedient history.

WILD GEESE ALIGHTING ON A LAKE

I watched them
As they neared the lake

They wheeled
In a wide arc
With beating wings
And then

They put their wings to sleep
And glided downward in a drift
Of pure abandonment

Until they touched
The surface of the lake

Composed their wings
And settled
On the rippling water
As though it were a nest.

LISTENING TO THE CROWS

Infant in a pinewood
Lying in a basket
Not owning anything
Not knowing
A single word

I listened to the shiny
Crows outside my window
As they spoke with one another
In a strange tribal language

And even now
When I wake up early
And overhear the crows
Calling to one another
In the cool floods of the air

The deeps of infancy
Open within me
Their wonder washes me
And instantly

My heart grows light
As light as if the world
Had never fallen.

THE BIRDS OF PASSAGE

You are the one who made us
You silver all the minnows in all rivers
You wait in the deep woods
To find the newborn fox cubs
And unseal their eyes
You shower the sky with stars

You walk alone
In the wild royal darkness
Of the heavens above the heavens
Where no one else can go.

When the fragile swallows assemble
For their pilgrimages
When the hummingbirds
Who are scarcely more
Than a glittering breath
Set out for the rain forest
To drink from the scarlet flowers
On the other side of the world
With only now and then
The mast of a passing ship
For a resting place and an inn

When the Canada geese
Are coming down from the north
When the storks of Europe
Stretch out their necks toward Egypt
From their nests on the chimney tops
When shaking their big wings open
And trailing their long legs after them

They rise up heavily
To begin their autumn flight

You who speak without words
To your creatures who live without words
Are hiding under their feathers

To give them a delicate certainty
On the long dangerous night journey.

THE WALL

I'm on a journey
And looking out the window of the train
At signs of early spring
Some of the trees
Have put forth flakes of leaf
Translucent, pale from winter
And the young rye
Is downy on the furrows
The sky is overcast
There's little color

It must be windy out
Rivers and bays
Are chipped and chiseled with small waves
Here is a lake
And on it is a fleet of swans
Bending their necks to feed
Or slowly sailing

Their ancestors
Were brought from England
To ornament the waters
Of country mansions
But now they have gone wild and multiplied
They nest in solitary places
Of their own choosing
It's there I've seen them
Shining like angels in the reedy ponds
Of the salt marshes near the sea

And now we're coming to a station
Where I look up

And see a high retaining wall
Of rough-cut stone

And near the top of the wall
There are three words
That have been carefully written with black paint
I have just time to read them
The words are DIGNITY IN PESTILENCE.

A BIOGRAPHY OF FLOWERS

This is the history of three small brown onions
Each had two poles, at one
A fringe of dried-up rootlets
And opposite
An inch-long leaf bud like an ivory fang.
I took them home
And stood them in a bowl of stones and water
And closed them up in a dark place.

Living for days on nothing but water and darkness
The rootlets thickened and the leaf buds grew.
I brought them out to the bare winter sunshine
Where fed by light as flames by air
The leaves flowed high and filled themselves with green
Then at their tips
Like the green heads of many little serpents
Each blindfolded by a tight filmy sheath
The flower buds appeared,

Enlarged, grew lumpy, split,
Till lightly as a snake's shed skin
The stripéd bud cases peeled off.

Then on the cloudy morning
Of February's eleventh day
There opened with birth's dazzling shock
And all in silence

Immaculate white flowers.

FOR THE TWO KATHERINES

On the last days of May
And the first days of June
We walked through the clear green shadows
Of the horse-chestnut trees
When they were all in flower.

The buds were shedding their husks
Shiny and brown as the pastries
In the bakeshop window
And shaped like beetles' wings
They were lying all over the sidewalk
And they stuck to our shoes.

❖   ❖   ❖

It's near the feast of Pentecost
And always at this season
The horse-chestnut trees
Keep their own festival
Whose calendar is hidden
In the depths of the sun.

All around the parks
And all through the villages
Under sun and moon
And falling rain
They hold up by the hundreds
Their torches heaped with flowers.

❖   ❖   ❖

High in the chestnut trees
The blossoms on their spindles
Appear a woolly white

But when I was a child
And found some of the blossoms
Loosened, fallen
And caught in the grass,
Their threads of gold astonished me

And every flower was signed
With four small spots of crimson
That filled me
With a mysterious joy.

THE PEAR TREE

Today the ninety-year-old pear tree
In my neighbors' garden
Stricken with petals
Is white all over
Startling as a cry

Its every branch and shoot
Spur twig and spray
Has broken into blossom

And every blossom
Is flinging itself open
Wide open

Disclosing every tender filament
Sticky with nectar
Beaded with black pollen.

WHEN THE PRIVET BLOOMS

In their green innocence
The privet bushes
Planted as hedges
Around the great estates

Are hedges unawares

But they have deciphered the sun
And they can read
The windy seaside rain

And just at midsummer
They know it's time
To bear
Their whitish blossoms

Then the hedge cutters come
And climb on ladders
To shear off the new growth
And with it all the flowers

But on the overgrown
Untended bushes
Around the edges
Of neglected meadows

You still may find
Those little spikes of blossom
With their delicious fragrance

That's partly like sweet chocolate
And a bit like rubber.

ON MY MOTHER'S BIRTHDAY

The thunderstorm is over
The grey cloud cover
Has been dismantled
The broken clouds
Are bundled off together
Leaving a clear blue sky

The pear tree is in blossom
Dark purple buds are forming
On lilac bushes
The star-of-Bethlehem
And buttercups
Are just beginning
To open in the grass

Lighter than air the small
White cabbage butterflies
Are lifted as they dance
And now for the first time
Since winter ended
I hear the tumbling
Music of the wren

Innocent messengers
You have split winter open
And brought us
Your transparent beauty

That's doubly beautiful
Because you're not like us
Because you cannot lie.

ANOTHER SARAH

for Christopher Smart

When winter was half over
God sent three angels to the apple tree
Who said to her
"Be glad, you little rack
Of empty sticks,
Because you have been chosen.

In May you will become
A wave of living sweetness
A nation of white petals
A dynasty of apples."

HOUSE LOTS

Good-bye lustrous pheasant
And pheasant's brown wife
Good-bye black-eyed Susan
And purple loosestrife

Good-bye sweet-whistling quail
Milkweed and Queen Anne's lace
Good-bye shy cottontail
Quit your secret room
Your burrow is for sale
The bulldozers have come.

A VILLAGE CAT

At the old Polish gardener's
There's a young cat
A calico
Living half-wild
Under the potting shed
Where she was born

Her face is decorated
With daubs and smudges
And streaks of black
As if she were made up to be a clown
In some mysterious carnival

I gaze at her in wonder
She gazes back
With her clear golden eyes.

LA TRANSHUMANCE

Through towns and over bridges
And into country lanes
A man and his dog are guiding
A jostling flock of sheep

Always in front of them
Still far away
But growing nearer
Is the serene mountain

All its deep snows
Have melted into streams
A wealth of new pasture
Has been laid bare

In those high meadows
Where clouds are at home
The sheep will graze

And up there too
Certain as a star
Is the shepherd's hut

My friend who grew up
On a farm in France
Is trying to remember
The word they have for it
What it is they call it

When spring comes and the sheep
Are led up into the mountains.

FOR DAVID

for David Shapiro

Here open at our feet
There lies a bottomless
Abyss of evil

A wound so deep
That at the sight of it
The spirit
Freezes within us

For though it was not You
But we ourselves
Who dug this dreadful grave
You did not stop us

Why
Have You permitted it

This is a gulf so wide
There's no way round it

A swamp so venomous
That no one
Can wade through it

There's no bridge over it
How
Can we reach
Our country

Unless You lift us up
Onto Your shoulders
And carry us across
O Lord our Shepherd

LA COURTE PAILLE

When our ship was sinking
And we were going to drown
The little cabin boy
Said I'm going to climb
Right up to the top of the mast

So he climbed up the rigging
As high as he could go
And we could hear him singing:

There's the coast of Barbary
Over to one side of us
And on the other side of us
The towers of Babylon

And now I see the hills
The hills of my own country
What are those white clouds
Floating all over the hills
In my own country

O those must be the apple trees
The orchards are in bloom

And there's my mother standing
Alone at the door
I'll get the morning stars
To come and sing for her

The way they sang together
On the first of all mornings.

—(PARTLY) FROM AN OLD FRENCH BALLAD

HOUSEGUESTS

"All of us are coming"
No they are not coming
They may be coming
They may not be coming.

Four of them are coming,
That is, if they are coming!
Five will come on Friday
Three will leave on Sunday
Two will come back Tuesday,
That is, if they are coming.

If they were coming
Two of them would be coming
But they are not coming . . .

Six of them are coming!

THE TICKET

On the night table
Beside my bed
I keep a small
Blue ticket

One day I found it
In my pocketbook
I don't know how
It got there

I don't know
What it's for

On one side
There's a number
98833
And
INDIANA TICKET COMPANY

And on the other side
The only thing it says
Is KEEP THIS TICKET

I keep it carefully
Because I'm old
Which means
I'll soon be leaving
For another country

Where possibly
Some blinding-bright
Enormous angel

Will stop me
At the border

And ask
To see my ticket.

AUTUMN CROCUS

Some of the leaves
Are falling early
But there are glinting
Dragonflies
Hornets in windfalls
And a brown honeybee
Searching about
In the surviving roses

The summer birds
Are just beginning
Their autumn journeys

We watch
Their clustered flocks
Unraveling in the sky
And always rising
Until they trail away
As small as gnats
And higher than the sun

We watch them out of sight
The air
Is drained of summer

We're left behind
With apple-scented nights
With carillons of crickets
With planets bright
As the Nativity

And this new air
Whose coolness is itself
A kind of fragrance

And now the earth
Breathes out the unearthly blossoms
Of the autumn crocus
Around the toolshed door.